Anonymous

Manual of the Public Schools of the City of Indianapolis

Anonymous

Manual of the Public Schools of the City of Indianapolis

ISBN/EAN: 9783337290900

Printed in Europe, USA, Canada, Australia, Japan

Cover: Foto ©Paul-Georg Meister /pixelio.de

More available books at **www.hansebooks.com**

MANUAL

OF THE

PUBLIC SCHOOLS

OF THE

CITY OF INDIANAPOLIS.

RULES AND REGULATIONS

OF THE

Board of School Commissioners;

OF THE

PUBLIC SCHOOLS;

AND THE

PUBLIC LIBRARY.

1879–80.

INDIANAPOLIS:
WM. B. BURFORD, PRINTER AND BINDER.

1879.

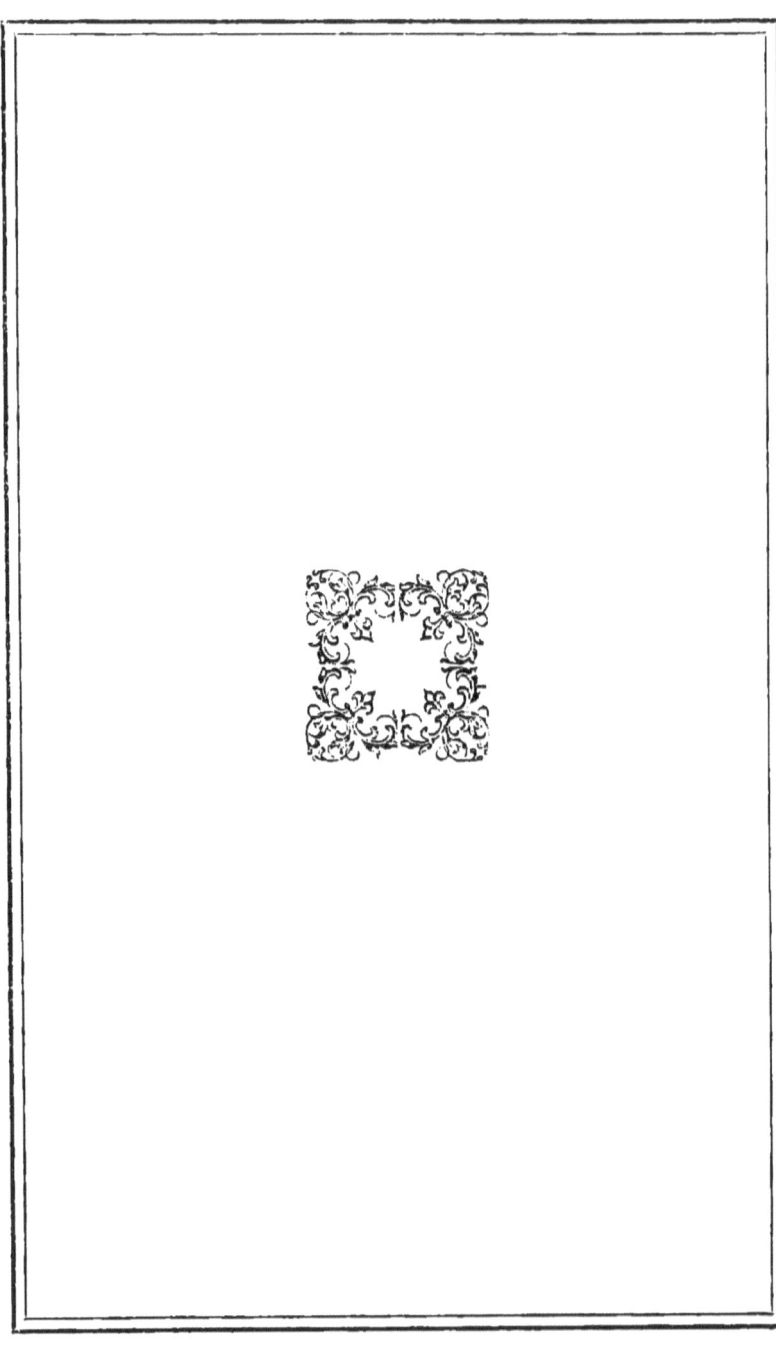

CALENDARS FOR THE YEARS 1879-80.

Officers of the Board.

PRESIDENT,
W. A. BELL.

SECRETARY,
JOSEPH J. BINGHAM.

TREASURER,
H. G. CAREY.

SUPERINTENDENT OF SCHOOLS,
H. S. TARBELL.

CLERK,
JOHN R. GIBSON.

BUILDING AND SUPPLY AGENT,
H. C. HENDRICKSON.

MESSENGER,
EDWARD CROSLEY.

Office in Library Building, corner Meridian and Circle streets. Open from 7½ A. M. to 6 P. M.

Office of H. C. Hendrickson, Building and Supply Agent, in office of Board, where orders intended for him may be left. Office hours from 8 to 9 o'clock A. M.

The Officers and Janitors will be paid on the last day of each month, unless it should occur on Sunday, but in that case on the day previous.

Standing Committees.

Finance and Auditing,
Merritt, Routier, and Vonnegut.

Buildings and Grounds,
Browning, Routier, Vonnegut, Merritt, and Brown.

Furniture and Supplies,
Routier, Brown, and Reasner.

Text-Books and Course of Instruction,
Carey, Brown, and Hyde.

Examination of Teachers and Schools,
President, Superintendent, Reasner, and Hyde.

Appointment of Teachers and Salaries.
Brown, Carey, and Vonnegut.

High School, Training School, and Night Schools,
Smith, Bingham, and Merritt.

German, Music, and Drawing,
Vonnegut, Smith, and Bingham.

Heating, Ventilation, and Janitors,
Bingham, Vonnegut, and Browning.

Judiciary, Discipline, and Boundaries,
Reasner, Smith, and Merritt.

Public Library,
Hyde, Bingham, Browning, and Carey.

Citizens' Advisory Library Committee,
Oscar C. McCulloch, C. C. Hines, Mrs. M. N. McKay, and Mrs. India Harris.

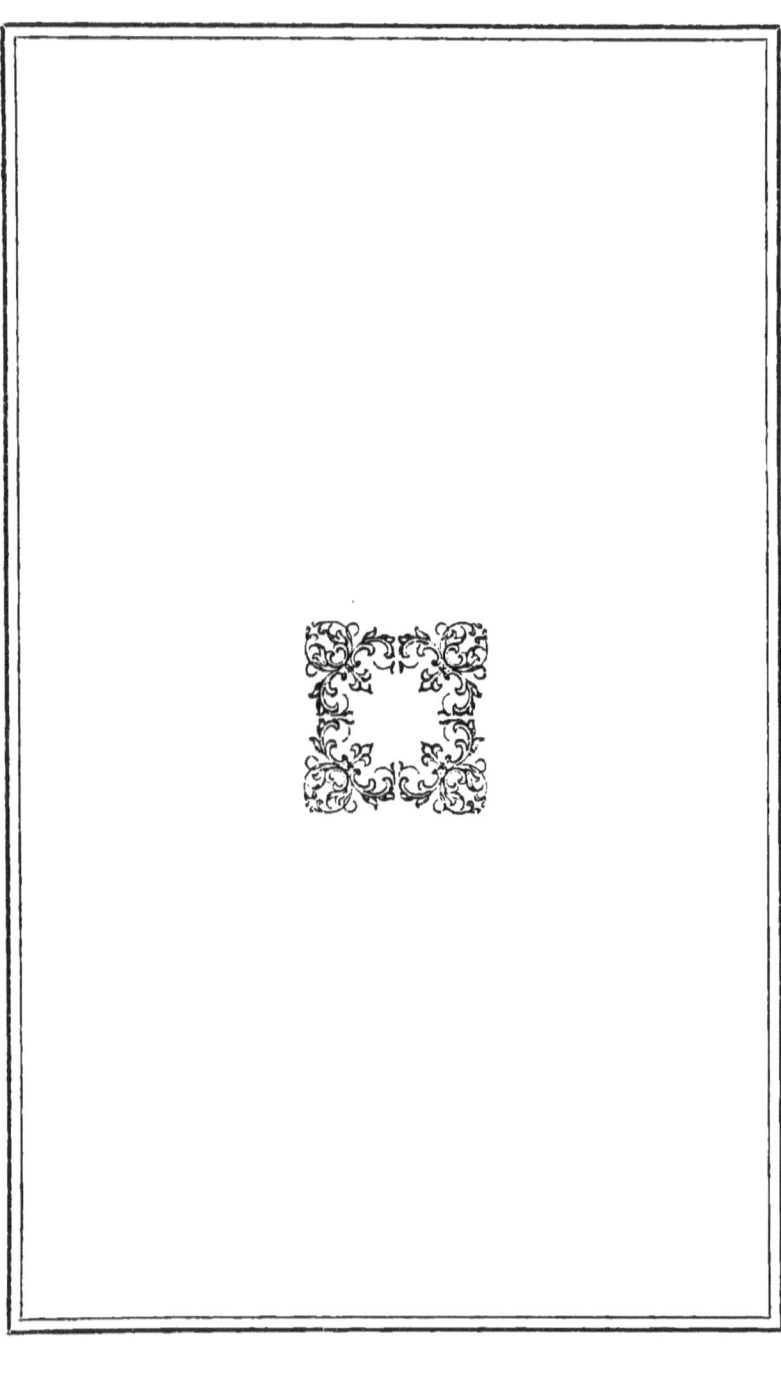

RULES FOR THE GOVERNMENT

OF THE

Board of School Commissioners

OF THE CITY OF INDIANAPOLIS.

ARTICLE I.

ORGANIZATION OF BOARD—ELECTION OF OFFICERS.

SECTION 1. The law establishing the Board of School Commissioners provides that the Board shall organize on the first Monday in July by "electing one of their number as a President, one of their number as a Treasurer, and one of their number as a Secretary, each of which officers shall serve for one year, and until his successor is elected and qualified." The Board shall elect at the same time and for the same term, a Superintendent of Schools, a Clerk, a Building and Supply Agent, and a Messenger. The election of officers shall be by ballot, and a majority of all the votes cast shall be necessary to a choice.

ARTICLE II.

DUTIES OF PRESIDENT.

SECTION 1. It shall be the duty of the President to preside at all meetings of the Board; preserve order; rigidly enforce the rules; sign all bonds, notes, agreements, deeds, mortgages, and other documents ordered to be executed by the Board; appoint all standing committees and all special committees, when not otherwise provided for; see that the requisitions of the laws for the government of the schools be presented to the members of the Board at the proper period for their action, and that the several committees discharge their respective duties; and perform such other duties as may properly appertain to his office, or be enjoined upon him by the Board.

ARTICLE III.

DUTIES OF SECRETARY.

SECTION 1. It shall be the duty of the Secretary to take the general supervision of the books, accounts and papers of the Board; to deposit in a safe place all documents that require preservation, subject at all times to the order of the Board or the examination of any member thereof; to draw warrants upon the Treasurer for all bills, salaries and allowances authorized by the Board or approved by the Finance and

Auditing Committe; to see that the office business of the Board is properly and promptly executed; to report at the end of each month a list of all warrants drawn upon the Treasurer and the funds to which they are chargeable; to make out at the end of the fiscal year a report of the financial condition of the Board, with a statement of the situation of the property in its possession and an estimate of the expenditures for the next fiscal year, and such other duties as may be required by law or enjoined upon him by the Board.

ARTICLE IV.

DUTIES OF TREASURER.

SECTION 1. It shall be the duty of the Treasurer "to give bond in such sum and with such surety as the Board may determine for the faithful discharge of his duties, and for the safe keeping and accounting for all moneys that may come into his hands as such Treasurer;" to keep a record of his receipts and disbursements in a book to be kept by him, which shall at all times be subject to the inspection of the Board or any of its members; to report to the Board at the end of each month a detailed statement of receipts and disbursements during the month, with the balances to the debit or credit of the different funds, whenever required; to report to the Board at its meeting on the first Monday in July of each year the receipts and disbursements of the fiscal year ending June 30, with the condition of the different funds; to disburse the funds in his hands upon the warrants of the Secretary of the Board, and in no other way, and such other duties as may be enjoined upon him by law and the Board.

ARTICLE V.

DUTIES OF CLERK

SECTION 1. It shall be the duty of the Clerk to keep a correct record of the proceedings of the Board in a book kept for that purpose, and an index to the same; to keep such books and in such forms and under such headings as the Board from time to time directs; to file all reports and communications that are accepted by the Board. It shall be his duty, under the direction of the Committee on Furniture and Supplies, to make all purchases after the commencement of the school year of supplies other than janitor's supplies; he shall have charge of the supply room of the Board, and all supplies to the several schools shall be issued by him upon the order of the principals, provided that all orders for janitor's supplies shall be approved by the Building and Supply Agent, and orders for all other supplies, including text-books for teachers, books for indigent children and books and apparatus for night schools, shall be approved by the First Assistant Superintendent. He shall keep an itemized account of the purchase and distribution of each kind of supplies, charging said account with the amount purchased and crediting it with the amounts issued, and at the close of the year he shall make a report to the Board in the form of a balance sheet, showing the amount of each kind of supplies on hand at the close of the preceding year, the amount purchased, and the amount issued during the year to each building, with the cost of the same, and the balance on hand in the several school houses and the supply room. It shall be his duty to notify members of the Board of special meetings called according to the rules, and of changes in the time of regular meetings; to take general charge of the rooms of the Board and the property contained therein; to be present at the office from 8 A. M. to 12 M., and from 1 to 5½ P. M.; to transmit copies of all votes, resolutions and documents which are to be sent to the members of the Board, to the various committees, to the teachers, or to other persons; to call together committees when ordered by their respective chairmen; to receive, have properly authenticated, and record all bills against the Board, and present the same by 2 o'clock on bill day to the Finance and Auditing Committee, the bills not presented at that time to be laid over until next bill day; to give such assistance to the Superintendent of Schools in the discharge of his official and clerical duties as he may require, and such other duties as may be enjoined upon him by the Board.

ARTICLE VI.

DUTIES OF SUPERINTENDENT.

Section 1. The Superintendent of Schools shall act under the advice and direction of the Board, and shall have superintendence of all the public schools, and of all the teachers and assistants, record books, blanks, etc , and the apparatus intended for instruction in the schools. He shall devote himself exclusively to the duties of his office. He shall attend all meetings of the Board, and, when requested, those of the Standing Committees. He shall be present every day at the office of the Board, between the hours of 4½ and 5½ o'clock P. M , to attend to such office business as pertains to his department, except when absent by consent of the Board. He shall direct and, as far as possible, supervise the details of instruction in all the public schools of the city. He shall visit the schools as often as practicable, note the manner by which their defects may be obviated and their efficiency promoted, and if, under the existing rules of the Board, it be not within his power to apply the necessary remedies, he shall recommend to the Board such changes in the rules and government to accomplish that end, with such other measures as to him may seem advisable.

Sec. 2. He shall keep a registry of the names and address of all applicants for employment as teachers, and of the situations applied for respectively, and shall cause notices to be given to such applicants, stating the time and the place for the examination of candidates, and notify the teachers of their appointment. In connection with the Committee on Examination of teachers, he shall examine all applicants for situations as teachers, keep a record of such examination, and report the result to the Committee on the Appointment of Teachers with his recommendations.

Sec. 3. It shall be the duty of the Superintendent, conjointly with the Committee on the Appointment of Teachers, to fill all vacancies occasioned by temporary illness or necessary absence of teachers; to make other temporary arrangements relative to the schools which he may deem proper, and report the same to the Board at its first subsequent meeting. He shall attend the examinations of the schools, and assist in the same concurrently with the committee and teachers under whose direction they take place. He shall see that all the necessary school registers, books of record and blanks for the use of the teachers, are prepared and ready to be furnished when needed. He shall certify to the monthly pay rolls of the teachers, and shall assist the Treasurer in paying the same.

Sec. 4. In the location, building and alteration of school houses, it shall be his duty to communicate to the Committee on Buildings and Grounds such information upon the subject as he may possess, and shall suggest such plans for the same as he may consider best for the health and convenience of teachers and pupils, and most economical to the Board.

SEC. 5. He shall make inquiry as to the number and the condition of the children of the city who are not receiving the benefits of education, and shall endeavor to ascertain the reasons, and to suggest and apply the remedies. He shall also visit the private or independent schools of the city once in each year to ascertain their condition and such facts in regard to the same as may be of public benefit.

SEC. 6. At the first meeting of the Board in January of each year, the Superintendent shall report to the Board an estimate of the probable number of additional school children for whom seats should be provided before the month of September in the same year, specifying the localities in which the school accommodations are inadequate. He shall make an annual report as soon as possible after the close of every scholastic year, and not later than by the first day of October next ensuing.

SEC. 7. He shall fix the time and prescribe the mode of all examinations of pupils for promotion from class to class, and from the primary to the high school, determine the conditions thereof so that they may be equal and uniform throughout all the schools. In the performance of this duty he may require the aid of such teachers as he may call on for the purpose. He shall meet the teachers at stated periods during term time, for the purpose of instructing them in the theory and practice of teaching and the best means of governing their schools. And he shall discharge such other duties as the Board shall from time to time direct.

ARTICLE VII.

DUTIES OF BUILDING AND SUPPLY AGENT.

SECTION 1. It shall be the duty of this officer to superintend the building of school houses, the out-buildings and fences, and all repairs made to the same, and he shall have general oversight and care of all the grounds and buildings under the control of the Board. In the purchase of materials and supplies for his department, including supplies for Janitors, he shall be under the general direction of the Committees on Buildings and Grounds, on Furniture and Supplies, on Heating, Ventilation and Janitors, and the Superintendent of Schools. At the end of the school year he shall make, in conjunction with the principals at the several school buildings and the clerk at the supply room of the Board, an inventory showing the amount and condition of supplies remaining on hand in the several buildings and in the supply room, which inventory he shall file with the clerk; and he shall also present to the Board at its first regular meeting in July a statement showing the amount of all kinds of supplies on hand at the beginning of the fiscal year, the amount purchased, the amount issued during the year, and the amount on hand as shown by the above named inventory and account as far as possible for all deficiencies and discrepancies. He shall make contracts with the Janitors under the direction of the Committee on Heating, Ventilation and Janitors, and shall see that the janitors faithfully discharge their duties. He shall see that the arrangements for heating and ventilating the school houses are sufficient and kept in good order. During the summer vacation he shall have the school grounds, buildings, out houses and fences put in good order, and during the school term kept so, and he shall be subject to such other duties as the Board may prescribe.

ARTICLE VIII.

DUTIES OF MESSENGER.

SECTION 1. The messenger shall be subject to the direction of the Superintendent and Clerk; he shall keep the offices of the Board in order; he shall aid in the discharge of the clerical and office duties of the Superintendent and Clerk, and discharge such other duties as the board may prescribe.

ARTICLE IX.

STANDING COMMITTEES

Section 1. The standing committees shall be appointed by the President at the first regular meeting of the Board in July, after the first Monday, to be constituted as follows, and subject to the approval of the Board:

1. Finance and Auditing, three members.
2. Buildings and Grounds, five members.
3. Furniture and Supplies, three members.
4. Text Books and Course of Instruction, three members.
5. Examination of Teachers and Schools, the President, Superintendent and two members.
6. Appointment of Teachers and Salaries, three members.
7. High School, Training School and Night Schools, three members.
8. Public Library, four members and an advisory committee of four citizens.
9. German, Music and Drawing, three members.
10. Heating, Ventilation and Janitors, three members.
11. Judiciary, Discipline, and Boundaries, three members.

Finance and Auditing.

Sec. 2. It shall be the duty of this committee to meet upon the first and third Fridays of each month, at 2 o'clock P M., to audit the bills presented against the Board, and report the same to the Board that night.

All bills presented for auditing shall be countersigned by the chairman of the proper committee, or authority which gave the order for the same. Separate bills shall be rendered for the furniture, repairs, and current expenses of each school.

All extra work on buildings erected under contract must be reported to and sanctioned by the Board before the bills for such work shall constitute a proper voucher for the officers of the Board.

The monthly bills for the pay of teachers, officers, and janitors shall be paid upon their being approved by the Finance and Auditing Committee; such bills to be reported at the next regular meeting of the Board.

The committee shall, annually, at the last regular meeting in July, recommend to the Board the assessments to be levied for the different funds.

At the end of each fiscal year the committee shall examine the vouchers upon which warrants have been drawn, to see that they correspond with the warrants issued by the Secretary, and that they have been properly authenticated.

Buildings and Grounds.

SEC. 3. It shall be the duty of this committee to have general charge of all the grounds, buildings, out-houses, and improvements in possession of the

Board, and of all repairs and improvements ordered by the Board; to purchase grounds for school houses, under the direction and subject to the approval of the Board; to procure plans for new buildings, and have charge of the same while being erected, and to recommend any changes or improvements in the school buildings and grounds that it may regard necessary or advantageous.

Sec. 4. The committee shall report in February of each year such plans for the erection and enlargement of school houses as it may deem necessary to meet the increased demands for school room by the month of September in the next school year.

Sec. 5. The committee shall, in the months of June and December, and oftener, if required, examine into the state of the buildings belonging to the Board, and report what fixtures, painting, repairs or alterations may be required, and furnish an estimate of the cost of the same, and no repairs, the cost of which exceeds one hundred dollars, shall be allowed without the sanction of the committee and the order of the Board.

Furniture and Supplies.

Sec. 6. It shall be the duty of this committee to recommend the purchase of such apparatus as may be found necessary, and the purchase, change, or alteration of school furniture as it may deem expedient. At a regular meeting of the Board in July of each year it shall present to the Board an estimate of the amount of supplies of every kind to be provided by the Board for the use of teachers, pupils, and janitors of the public schools during the ensuing year; and, with the approval of the Board, it shall make contracts for the purchase of the same. It shall also exercise a supervision over all subsequent purchases of supplies during the year, and in all cases wherein it is practicable, sealed proposals for the furnishing of supplies, together with samples of the same, shall be taken and considered by the committee.

Text-Books and Course of Instruction.

SEC. 7. It shall be the duty of this committee, annually, at the first regular meeting of the Board in April, to make a report embracing such facts and suggestions in regard to text-books and course of instruction as it may think advisable to present. At this meeting any member may propose changes in text-books. All propositions for changes in text-books shall lie over for one month, when they may be acted upon. It shall not be in order for any commissioner at any other time to propose changes in text-books used in the schools, except by a vote of at least two-thirds of all the members of the Board. No text-book shall be considered as adopted, unless there shall be a concurrent vote of a majority of all the commissioners in its favor. All changes in text-books shall take effect only at the commencement of the fall term of the schools, unless it be otherwise ordered by a vote of two-thirds of all the members of the Board.

Examination of Teachers and Schools.

SEC. 8. It shall be the duty of this committee to examine all candidates who may apply for situations in the public schools. Examinations shall be held whenever, in the judgment of the committee, it is necessary. Candidates shall be examined in the absence of all spectators except the commissioners. It shall adopt such rules in regard to the examination of teachers as it may judge proper. A record of examinations shall be kept for the inspection of the Board. It shall also be the duty of this committee to examine the schools once during the scholastic year, and oftener if practicable; notice the discipline of the teachers and the progress of the pupils, and report to the Board the result of its examinations, with such suggestions as to changes or improvements in the management of the schools as it may deem advisable.

Appointment of Teachers and Salaries.

SEC. 9. At the first meeting of the Board in the month of June, annually, this committee shall report to the Board the appointment of teachers in the several schools, and fix their salaries for the ensuing year, subject to the approval of the Board. It shall, conjointly with the Superintendent, make nominations to fill new situations whenever they occur, subject to the approval of the Board. It shall have power, in conjunction with the Superintendent, to transfer teachers from one school to another, the principal of the school first being notified of the transfer, and to make temporary appointments in cases of vacancies occurring; but such changes and appointments shall be reported to the Board at its next meeting for its final decision.

High School, Training School, and Night Schools.

SEC. 10. This committee, with the Superintendent, shall have general supervision of these schools, subject to the approval of the Board. It shall be the duty of the committee to visit, as often as practicable, these schools, examine into the discipline and mode of instruction of each teacher, note the progress made by the several classes, and report to the Board at the end of each year their condition, with such suggestions for their improvement as it may deem advisable.

Public Library.

SEC. 11. This committee shall have general charge of all matters appertaining to the Public Library, but the action of the committee shall be reported to the Board and subject to its approval.

The committee shall, at the meeting of the Board preceding the annual meeting on the first Monday of July, in each year, nominate a Librarian, which nomination, upon the concurrence of a majority of the members of the Board at the annual meeting, shall be effective as an appointment.

In case of non concurrence with such nomination, the committee shall, at the next meeting of the Board, make other nominations subject to the approval of the Board as aforesaid.

The Librarian shall have the privilege of nominating his assistants for appointment by the committee, and the committee shall fix their compensation; the appointments and compensation to be subject to the approval of the Board.

The committee shall have power to suspend the Librarian or assistants at any time, subject to the approval of the Board at its first meeting thereafter.

The Librarian and assistants shall be subject to removal at any time, on the action of the committee, approved by a majority of the members of the Board.

The committee shall hold at least monthly meetings, the Librarian to act as secretary of the committee, and keep a record of its proceedings. The committee shall direct the purchase of books and all matters pertaining to the addition, improvement, regulation and management of the Library and Reading Rooms, and this committee shall report quarterly to the Board the condition of the Library, with such suggestions in regard thereto as it may deem practicable. No account or bill for books purchased for the Public Library shall be audited unless certified by the chairman of the committee and setting forth that the books were ordered by the committee.

The Advisory Committee of citizens shall be invited to attend the stated meetings of the committee for consultation in regard to all matters affecting the interests of the Library.

German, Music and Drawing.

SEC. 12. This committee, with the Superintendent, shall have general charge of instruction in the German Language, Music and Drawing; it shall recommend to the committe on the appointment of Teachers, such persons as it may find best fitted to teach the German Language, Music and Drawing when appointments are to be made, suggest text-books, and report quarterly to the Board the condition and wants of these departments in the schools.

Heating, Ventilation and Janitors.

SEC. 13. It shall be the duty of this committee to attend to the heating and ventilation of the school buildings; to recommend to the Board the purchase or change of furnaces, stoves or heating apparatus; to regulate, alter and prescribe the duties of the several janitors of the school houses, and to recommend to the Board their compensation; in connection with the Building and Supply Agent to appoint the janitors, requiring in all cases, previous to appointment, satisfactory evidence of integrity and capability to perform the duties of the position, and report its action to the Board for its approval.

Judiciary, Discipline and Boundaries.

Sec. 14. It shall be the duty of this committee to consider and report upon all questions submitted to it by the Board, and to suggest to the Board from time to time such changes in the boundaries of the several districts, and the addition of new districts, as it may deem advisable for the promotion of the educational interests of the city.

ARTICLE X.

MISCELLANEOUS.

Section 1. The Board shall hold meetings on the first and third Friday evenings of each month, and the sessions shall commence from and including October to May at 7½ o'clock, and from and including May to October at 8 o'clock. The President shall call the Board to order promptly at the hour designated for each meeting.

Sec. 2. A majority of the Board shall be requisite to constitute a quorum for the transaction of business, but a less number may vote to send for absent members, or to adjourn.

Sec. 3. The following shall be the order of business at the regular meetings of the Board:

    I. Roll call.
   II. Reading of minutes.
  III. Reports of officers.

IV. Reports and suggestions from Superintendent.
V. Communications.
VI. Reports of committees, standing and special.
VII. Special orders.
VIII. Unfinished business.
IX. New and miscellaneous business.

Sec. 4. No other business shall be done at the special meetings, except that which is designated in the call for the same.

Sec. 5. Whenever, in his opinion, it is necessary, the President *may*, and at the written request of three members the President *shall*, call a special meeting of the Board; but no meeting of the Board shall be called on shorter notice than twenty-four hours, unless some exigency occurs requiring more prompt action.

Sec 6. The President shall have a vote upon all questions; and whenever the vote shall be a tie, the motion pending shall be considered lost.

Sec. 7. The Clerk shall, at every meeting of the Board, furnish the President a list of reports due, the special orders, and all items of unfinished business, in the order of their appearance upon the minutes.

Sec 8. No motion shall be considered by the Board unless seconded. Reports and resolutions must be presented in writing, and every motion for disposal of business shall be submitted in writing, if the President so directs, or other members of the Board request it.

Sec 9. Every member present when a question

is put, shall give his vote, unless excused by the Board, and the sense of the Board shall be taken by yeas and nays, and entered on record at the request of any member, if made before the vote shall be announced.

Sec. 10. Any rule may be suspended for the time being by a vote of two-thirds of all the members of the Board.

Sec. 11. Any and all questions arising, and not provided for by the rules of the Board, shall be decided according to the parliamentary rules and usages for the government of deliberative bodies.

Sec. 12. All resolutions and orders of the Board contrary to or inconsistent with any of the foregoing rules, are hereby repealed.

Sec. 13. None of the foregoing rules shall be repealed or altered unless two-thirds of all the members vote for the repeal or alteration, upon motion made in writing for that purpose at a previous meeting of the Board.

Boundaries of Districts

For Election of Commissioners.

First District.

Beginning at the intersection of Washington and Pennsylvania streets; thence north by the center of Pennsylvania street to Vermont street; thence east by the center of Vermont street to Delaware street; thence north by the center of Delaware street to Michigan street; thence east by the center of Michigan street to Alabama street; thence north by the center of Alabama street to North street; thence east by the center of North street to New Jersey street; thence north by the center of New Jersey street to St. Clair street; thence east by the center of St. Clair street to Chatham street; thence south by the center of Chatham and Liberty streets to the Union railway tracks; thence south-west by the line of these tracks to Delaware street; thence north by the center of Delaware street to Virginia avenue; thence northwest by the center of Virginia avenue to the place of beginning.

Second District.

Beginning at the intersection of Meridian and Vermont streets; thence east by the center of Vermont street to Delaware street; thence north by the center of Delaware street to Michigan street; thence east by the center of Michigan street to Alabama street; thence north by the center of Alabama street to North street; thence east by the center of North street to New Jersey street; thence north by the center of New Jersey street to St. Clair street; thence east by the center of St. Clair street to Park avenue; thence north by the center of Park avenue to Cherry street; thence west by the center of Cherry street to Ft. Wayne avenue; thence north-east by the center of Ft. Wayne avenue to St. Mary street; thence west by the center of St. Mary street and First street to Lafayette railroad track; thence south on the line of said railroad track to Walnut street; thence east by the center of Walnut street to Illinois street; thence south by the center of Illinois street to North street; thence east by the center of North street to Meridian street; thence south by the center of Meridian street to the place of beginning.

Third District.

Beginning at the intersection of Pennsylvania and Washington streets; thence north by the center of Pennsylvania street to Vermont street; thence west by the center of Vermont street to Meridian street;

thence north by the center of Meridian street to North street; thence west by the center of North street to Illinois street; thence north by the center of Illinois street to Walnut street; thence west by the center of Walnut street to Lafayette railroad track; thence south by the line of said track to Ohio street; thence east by center of Ohio street to Tennessee street; thence south by the center of Tennessee street to Washington street; thence east by the center of Washington street to Pennsylvania street to the place of beginning.

Fourth District.

Beginning at the intersection of Tennessee and Washington streets; thence north by the center of Tennessee street to Ohio street; thence west by the center of Ohio street to the Lafayette railroad track; thence north on the line of the Lafayette railroad track to First street; thence west on the center of First street and the donation line to the west corporation line; thence south by the corporation line to White river; thence eastwardly by White river and the center of Washington street to Tennessee street to the point of beginning.

Fifth District.

Beginning at the intersection of White river and Washington street; thence east by the center of Washington street to Virginia avenue; thence south-east by the center of Virginia avenue to Delaware street; thence south by the center of Delaware street to the Union railway tracks; thence south-west on the line of the Union railway tracks to Louisiana street; thence west by the center of Louisiana street to Tennessee street; thence south by the center of Tennessee street and the canal to the south corporation line; thence west on the south corporation line to White river; thence northwardly following the course of White river to the place of beginning, and all west of White river within the city limits.

Sixth District.

Beginning at a point where the Union railway tracks cross Alabama street; thence south by the center of Alabama street to McCarty street; thence east by the center of McCarty street to High street; thence south by the center of High street to Coburn street; thence east by the center of Coburn street to the first alley running south; thence south by the center of the alleys on the west line of Vajen's addition and between Wallace street and Franklin street to Yeiser street; thence east by the center of Yeiser street to Franklin street; thence south by the center of Franklin and a continuous line to the south corporation line; thence west on the south corporation line to the canal; thence north by the canal and the center of Tennessee street to the Union railway tracks; thence east by the Union railway tracks to Alabama street to the place of beginning.

Seventh District.

Beginning at a point where the Union railway tracks cross Alabama street; thence north-east on the line of said tracks to Washington street; thence east by the center of Washington street and the National Road to the east corporation line; thence south on the east corporation line to a line running west that will strike the center of Fletcher street; thence west by the center of Fletcher street to the intersection of Fletcher avenue and Dillon street; thence north-west by the center of Fletcher avenue to South street; thence west by the center of South street to East street; thence north by the center of East street to Louisiana street; thence west by the center of Louisiana street to Alabama street; thence north by the center of Alabama street to the Union railway tracks to the place of beginning.

Eighth District.

Beginning at the intersection of Alabama and Louisiana streets; thence east by the center of Louisiana street to East street; thence south by the center of East street to South street; thence east by the center of South street to Fletcher avenue; thence south east by the center of Fletcher avenue to its intersection with Dillon street; thence east by the center of

Fletcher street or the continuation of Fletcher avenue and a continuous line to Reid street; thence south on Reid street and the east corporation line to the south corporation line; thence west on the south corporation line to a line running north that will strike Franklin street; thence north by the center of Franklin street to Yeiser street; thence west by the center of Yeiser street to the alley between Wallace and Franklin streets; thence north by the center of the alleys between Wallace and Franklin streets and on the west of Vajen's addition to Coburn street; thence west by the center of Coburn street to High street; thence north by the center of High street to McCarty street; thence west by the center of McCarty street to Alabama street; thence north by the center of Alabama street to Louisiana street to the place of beginning.

Ninth District.

Beginning at the intersection of Chatham and St. Clair streets; thence south by the center of Chatham and Liberty streets to the Union railway tracks south of Washington street; thence north east on the line of said railway tracks to Washington street; thence east by the center of Washington street and the National road to the east corporation line; thence north on said corporation line to Pogue's Creek gravel road; thence west to the western boundary of the arsenal grounds; thence south on the western boundary of the arsenal grounds to a point due east of and opposite to St. Clair street; thence west from said point to St. Clair street; thence west by the center of St. Clair street to the place of beginning.

Tenth District.

Beginning at the intersection of Delaware street and the donation line; thence south by the center of Delaware street to St. Mary street; thence east by the center of St. Mary street to Fort Wayne avenue; thence southwest by the center of Fort Wayne avenue to Cherry street; thence east by the center of Cherry street to Park avenue; thence south by the center of Park avenue to St. Clair street; thence east by the center of St. Clair street and the line of the north boundary of the ninth district to the east corporation line; thence north on the east corporation line to the north corporation line; thence west by the north corporation line to Delaware street; thence south by the center of Delaware street to the place of beginning.

Eleventh District.

Beginning at the intersection of Delaware street with the donation line; thence west on the donation line by the center of First street, and on the donation line again to the west corporation line; thence north on the west corporation line to the north corporation line; thence east on the north corporation line to

Delaware street; thence south on Delaware street to the place of beginning.

The districts running to the corporation lines are bounded by the corporation lines, if the description of the boundaries of the districts does not so express it.

SCHOOLS IN DISTRICTS.

First District, No. 1.
Second District, No. 2.
Third District, Nos. 3 and 21.
Fourth District, Nos. 4, 15 and 24.
Fifth District, Nos. 5, 12 and 16.
Sixth District, Nos 6 and 22.
Seventh District, No. 7.
Eighth District, Nos. 8, 13, 19, 20 and 25.
Ninth District, Nos 9 and 14.
Tenth District, Nos. 10 and 18.
Eleventh District, Nos. 11, 17 and 23.

SCHOOL LAWS FOR CITIES

OF

30,000 OR MORE INHABITANTS.

AN ACT providing for a general system of Common Schools in all cities of thirty thousand or more inhabitants, and for the election of a Board of School Commissioners for such cities, and defining their duties and prescribing their powers, and providing for Common School Libraries within such cities.

[APPROVED MARCH 3, 1871.]

SECTION 1. *Be it enacted by the General Assembly of the State of Indiana,* That in all cities of this State, of thirty thousand or more inhabitants, according to the United States census for the year eighteen hundred and seventy, there shall be elected by the qualified electors of each school district of such city, one School Commissioner, to serve as a member of the Board of School Commissioners of such city. The first regular election for School Commissioners, under this act, shall be held on the second Saturday in June, in the year eighteen hundred and seventy-one, at the places to be fixed on for holding such election in the school district of such city by the Common Council. All elections for School Commissioners shall be held in the same manner as elections are now held, and shall be governed by the same laws that now govern general and municipal elections; and the persons declared elected shall have issued to them, by the City Clerk, certificates of election, and they shall, within ten days thereafter, take an oath of office, and file the same with the City Clerk. All regular elections for School Commissioners shall thereafter be held annually on the second Saturday in June.

SEC. 2. It is hereby made the duty of the Common council of any such city, on or before the first Monday in May, 1871, by ordinance, to district the city into as many school districts as there are wards, and to define the boundaries of each district, and such boundaries may be the present ward boundaries, or otherwise, as the Common Council may determine. Such school district shall, however be subject to change by the Board of School Commissioners at any time after its organization; and in case the number of districts is increased, each additional district shall be entitled to elect one School Commissioner for such district at the annual election for School Commissioners. And the Common Council shall, at the time such ordinance is adopted creating such districts, order an election to be held in each of such districts, for School Commissioner thereof, on the second Saturday in June following, and shall direct the City Clerk to give ten days notice thereof in some daily newspaper of such city.

Sec. 3 On the first Monday in July following the first election of School Commissioners herein provided for, such School Commissioners shall assemble at the office of the Board of School Trustees of such city, and proceed to organize the Board of School Commissioners of such city by electing one of their number as a President, one of their number as a Treasurer, and one of their number as a Secretary, each of which officers shall serve for one year, and until his successor is elected and qualified. The members of such Board of School Commissioners shall then determine, by lot, which three of their number shall hold office for three years, and which three shall hold office for two years; and after having so determined, the President of the Board shall issue to the persons so determined, certificates entitling them to hold office for the term respectively allotted, and the remaining members shall receive from the President of the Board certificates showing that each is entitled to hold office for one year; and all persons elected as School Commissioners at the annual elections thereafter shall be entitled to hold office for three years each. All vacancies occurring at any time prior to the annual election shall be filled by a ballot vote of a majority of the members of such Board, and the persons so elected to fill such vacancies shall serve until the next annual election for

School Commissioners. All persons elected at any regular annual election, or by the Board to fill any vacancy, shall serve until their successors are elected and qualified. It is hereby made the duty of the Board of School Trustees, in office at the time of the organization of the Board of School Commissioners, to at once turn over to the Board of School Commissioners all books and papers pertaining to their trust, and to place in possession of the Board of School Commissioners all moneys, title papers and property belonging to the School Trustees or Common Schools of such city, and such Board of School Trustees shall thereafter cease to perform any and all duties whatever connected with the schools of such city.

SEC. 4. Such Board of School Commissioners is hereby authorized:

1. To district the city for the purpose of electing School Commissioners therein, and also to subdivide the city for general school purposes.

2. To levy all taxes for the support of the schools within such city, including such taxes as may be required for paying teachers, in addition to the taxes now authorized to be evied by the General Assembly of this State by the general laws thereof: *Provided*, No such tax levy in any one year shall exceed the sum of twenty-five cents on each one hundred dollars of the taxable property as assessed for city taxes by the City Assessor, for purchasing grounds, building school houses, and furnishing supplies for such buildings, or twenty-five cents on each one hundred dol-

lars of such taxable property for the purpose of paying teachers.

3. To levy a tax each year of not exceeding one-fifth of one mill on each dollar of taxable property assessed for city taxes by the City Assessor for the support of free libraries in connection with the common schools of such city, and to disburse any and all revenue raised by such tax levy in the purchase of books for and in the fitting up of suitable rooms for such libraries, and for salaries to librarians; also to make and enforce such regulations as they may deem necessary for the taking out from and returning to, and for the proper care of all books belonging to such libraries, and to prescribe penalties for the violation of such regulations.

4. To examine, either by a committee of such Board of School Commissioners, or by an officer of such Board selected for that purpose, all teachers applying for positions in the schools of the city, and to license such as may be qualified, such license to be limited to the city in which the same is granted.

5. To purchase grounds, construct school buildings, purchase supplies, employ and pay teachers, appoint superintendents, and disburse, through the Treasurer of the Board of School Commissioners, moneys for all school and library expenses.

6. To require the Treasurer of the Board of School Commissioners to give bond in such sum, and with such surety as the Board may determine for the faithful discharge of his duties, and for the safe keep-

ing and faithful accounting for all moneys that may come into his hands as such treasurer.

7. To establish and enforce regulations for the grading of and course of instruction in the schools of the city, and for the government and discipline of such schools.

8. To prepare, issue, and sell bonds to secure loans not exceeding in the aggregate the sum of one hundred thousand dollars, in anticipation of the revenue for building school houses, to bear such rate of interest, not exceeding ten per cent. per annum, and payable at such time within five years from date as the Board may determine, and the money obtained as a loan on any such bonds, shall be disbursed by order of such Board, in payment of expenses incurred in building school houses; *Provided*, That until all the bonds of any one issue shall have been redeemed, such Board shall not be authorized to make another issue, nor shall any such bonds be sold at a less rate than ninety-five cents on the dollar.

SEC. 5. All levies of taxes made by order of the Board of School Commissioners shall be certified by its President and Secretary to the City Clerk, who shall cause the same to be placed on the tax duplicate against all property assessed for city taxes, and the City Treasurer shall collect the same as city taxes are collected, and shall once in each month pay over all such taxes so collected to the Treasurer of the Board of School Commissioners of such city. All taxes hereafter collected by the County Treasurer for school purposes on levies hereafter made, and all moneys that may be hereafter distributed as part of the common school fund by county officers to which the common schools of such city shall be entitled, shall be paid over by the Coun'y Treasurer to the Treasurer of the Board of School Commissioners, and all taxes hereafter collected by the City Treasurer on levies heretofore made for school purposes, shall be paid over by such Treasurer once in each month to the Treasurer of the Board [of] School Commissioners of such city.

SEC. 6. Such Board of School Commissioners shall hold its session at such times as it may determine, and shall keep a record of all its proceedings; and the members of such Board shall serve without any compensation whatever.

SEC. 7. * The Common Council of any city having a less population than thirty thousand inhabitants, may, by a majority vote of the members thereof, at any time, order the election of members of a Board of School Commissioners, according to the provisions of this act; which Board, when elected and organized shall have all the powers, and shall perform all the duties required by the provisions of this act, and shall supersede the Board of School Trustees then in office.

SEC. 8. All parts of the general school laws of this State not inconsistent herewith, and which may

---

* Unconstitutional.

be applicable to the general system of common schools in such city, herein provided for, shall be in full force and effect in such city. And all provisions of the general school laws inconsistent herewith be and the same are hereby repealed, so far as the same are applicable to common schools in any city having thirty thousand or more inhabitants.

SEC. 9. It is hereby declared that an emergency exists for the immediate taking effect of this act, therefore, this act is declared to be in force from and after its passage.

PUBLIC SCHOOLS.

Officers and Teachers.

Superintendent of Schools,
H. S. TARBELL,
890 N. Alabama street.

Clerk of Superintendent,
JOHN R. GIBSON.

Assistant Superintendents,

J. J. Mills, 226 College avenue	$1,800
Lewis H. Jones, 110 Plum street	1,200

Superintendent of Primary Instruction,

Miss N. Cropsey, 85 College avenue	$1,200

Supervisors of Special Branches,

Geo. B. Loomis, Music, 574 North Alabama street	$1,200
Jesse H. Brown, Drawing, 209 Broadway	1,350
Charles E. Emmerich, German, 251 North Liberty street	250

Offices of the Public Schools in the Sentinel Building.

OFFICE HOURS.

Superintendent, from 4½ to 5½ P. M. each week day.

Clerk, from 8 A. M. to 5½ P. M. each week day.

First Assistant Superintendent, 4½ to 5 P. M. each school day.

Second Assistant Superintendent, 4½ to 5 P. M. Monday, Wednesday and Friday.

Superintendent of Primary Instruction, 4½ to 5 P. M. Tuesday.

Supervisor of Drawing, 4½ to 5 P. M. Wednesday.
Supervisor of Music, 4½ to 5 P. M Thursday.
Supervisor of German, 4½ to 5 P. M. Friday.

Normal School,

In High School Building.

Lewis H. Jones, Principal, 110 Plum street .. $200
Armada G. Paddock, Assistant, 277 North Delaware street 950

HIGH SCHOOL.

Corner of Pennsylvania and Michigan Streets.

J. B. Roberts, 211 Park avenue, Principal..... $1,750
Eli F. Brown, 158 Broadway, Ass't Principal 1,200
A. W. Brayton, Irvington 950
C. E. Emmerich, 251 North Liberty street..... 950

Mary E. Nicholson, 232 Broadway	$950
James O. Wright, 799 North Tennessee street	950
Fidelia Anderson, 293 North Delaware street	950
May W. Thompson, 561 North Alabama street	950
Mary A. McGregory, 273 North Delaware street	950
Ellen F. Thompson, 743 North Tennessee street	850
Geo. W. Hufford, 427 North East street	800
A. W. Brayton, Curator of Museum	150

No 1.

Corner Vermont and New Jersey Streets.

Mary Colgan, Principal, 4 A B*, Room 1, 170 Christian avenue	700
Ida Zimmerman, 3 A B, Room 4, 566 East Washington street	400
Emma Coffman, 2 A B, Room 3, 97 North New Jersey street	480
Mary Altland, 1 A B, Room 2, 299 North Davidson street	480

No. 2.

Corner Delaware and Walnut Streets.

Herbert L. Rust, Principal, 8 B, Room 3, Remy Hotel	950
Lydia Halley, 7 A, Room 9, 16 East Michigan street	570

*The figures following the teacher's name indicate the year of school work being done by her class, 1 meaning first or lowest year; B signifying beginning or first half of the year's work, A advanced or second half of the year's work.

Ida Stearns, 7 B, Room 10, 288 Bellefontaine street..	$450
Rachel Hickey, 6 B, Room 11, 561 North Alabama street	530
Maggie Merrill, 5 A, Room 12, 154 North New Jersey street...............................	530
Adell Aldrich, 5 B, Room 5, 371 North Tennessee street..	400
Nannie T. Flanner, 4 A, Room 6, 230 East Vermont street.......................................	480
Kate E. Coffin, 4 B, Room 7, 410 North Pennsylvania street...................................	530
Fannie Jameson, 3 A, Room 8, 44 Cherry street	480
Hattie A. Scott, 3 B, Room 4, 254 North East street	480
Anna B. Keay, 2 B, Room 2, 378 North East street	480
Lottie Loyd, 1 A B, Room 1, 165 Park avenue...	530
Sophie C Dithmer, German, Room 14, 324 North Alabama street........................	530
William A. Geers, German, Room 15, 473 North Illinois street, (half day).............	200

No. 3.

Meridian Street, between Ohio and New York Streets.

George F. Bass, Principal, 8 A, Room 6, 367 College avenue......................................	950

PUBLIC SCHOOLS.

William H. Bass, 7 A and 8 B, Room 11, 318 North Delaware street	$570
Florence Fay, 7 B, Room 10, 446 North East street	570
Sadie Kirlin, 6 A, Room 4, 526 North Illinois street	530
Donia Allen, 6 B, Room 8, 132 West Vermont street	530
Frances Martin, 5 A, Room 7, 290 Christian avenue	450
Helen Hickey, 5 B, Room 9, 561 North Alabama street	480
Salome Waite, 4 A, Room 12, 373 North Delaware street	450
M. C. Tichenor, 4 B, Room 5	
Alice C. Tattersall, 3 A, Room 14, 40 English avenue	530
Hattie Cadwallader, 3 B, Room 3, 317 East Ohio street	480
Sallie Wells, 2 A B, Room 2, 119 North Illinois street	420
Mary Bass, 2 B, 1 A B, Room 1, 406 Ash street	450
Mary Avey, German, Room 15, 408 West North street	480

No. 4.

Corner of Michigan and Blackford Streets.

Eliza T. Ford, Principal, 8 A B, Room 1, 6 East Michigan street	950

Ida Stearns, 7 B, Room 10, 288 Bellefontaine street	$450
Rachel Hickey, 6 B, Room 11, 561 North Alabama street	530
Maggie Merrill, 5 A, Room 12, 154 North New Jersey street	530
Adell Aldrich, 5 B, Room 5, 371 North Tennessee street	400
Nannie T. Flanner, 4 A, Room 6, 230 East Vermont street	480
Kate E. Coffin, 4 B, Room 7, 410 North Pennsylvania street	530
Fannie Jameson, 3 A, Room 8, 44 Cherry street	480
Hattie A. Scott, 3 B, Room 4, 254 North East street	480
Anna B. Keay, 2 B, Room 2, 378 North East street	480
Lottie Loyd, 1 A B, Room 1, 165 Park avenue	530
Sophie C Dithmer, German, Room 14, 324 North Alabama street	530
William A. Geers, German, Room 15, 473 North Illinois street, (half day)	200

No. 3.

Meridian Street, between Ohio and New York Streets.

George F. Bass, Principal, 8 A, Room 6, 367 College avenue	950

PUBLIC SCHOOLS. 53

William H. Bass, 7 A and 8 B, Room 11, 318 North Delaware street	$570
Florence Fay, 7 B, Room 10, 446 North East street	570
Sadie Kirlin, 6 A, Room 4, 526 North Illinois street	530
Donia Allen, 6 B, Room 8, 132 West Vermont street	530
Frances Martin, 5 A, Room 7, 290 Christian avenue	450
Helen Hickey, 5 B, Room 9, 561 North Alabama street	480
Salome Waite, 4 A, Room 12, 373 North Delaware street	450
M. C. Tichenor, 4 B, Room 5	
Alice C. Tattersall, 3 A, Room 14, 40 English avenue	530
Hattie Cadwallader, 3 B, Room 3, 317 East Ohio street	480
Sallie Wells, 2 A B, Room 2, 119 North Illinois street	420
Mary Bass, 2 B, 1 A B, Room 1, 406 Ash street	450
Mary Avey, German, Room 15, 408 West North street	480

No. 4.

Corner of Michigan and Blackford Streets.

Eliza T. Ford, Principal, 8 A B, Room 1, 6 East Michigan street	950

A. William Geers, German, (half day,) 473
    North Illinois street $200

No. 7.

Corner of Bates and Benton Streets.

Nelson Yoke, Principal, 8 B, Room 8, 217
    Fletcher avenue 950
Kate A. Thompson, 7 B, Room 7, 277 Virginia avenue.. 570
M. Liggett, 6 B, Room 10, 166 North Mississippi street..
Mollie Z. Gilkison, 5 B, Room 9, 127 Meek
    street 420
Anna J. Griffith, 5 B, Room 12, 297 East McCarty street.. 480
Olive McElwee, 4 A, Room 11, 315 E. Ohio
    street 530
Augusta Byram, 4 B, Room 2, 110 West Vermont street.. 530
Augusta Gilkison, 3 A, Room 1, 127 Meek
    street 480
Anna Tattersall, 3 B, Room 4, 40 English avenue 480
Kate Rogers, 2 A, Room 3, 82 North Noble
    street... 480
Anna Homan, 2 B, Room 6, 154 South New
    Jersey street.. 480
Della Echols, 1 B, Room 5, 266 N. East st. 450
Mary Brueckner, German, Room 9, 154 North
    New Jersey street................................. 400

No. 8.

Virginia Avenue, corner Huron Street.

Delia Curtis, Principal, 1 B A and 2 B, Room 1, 300 South New Jersey......................	$700
A. B. Thomas, 5 B and 4 A, Room 3, 42 Fletcher avenue................................	530
Mattie Lannes, 4 B and 3 A, Room 5, 275 North Pine street..............................	480
Lucretia Hobart, 3 B and 2 A, Room 4, 277 Virginia avenue..............................	480

No. 9.

Corner Vermont and Davidson Streets.

Henrietta Schrake, Principal, 8 B, Room 1, 253 North Noble street......................	950
Anna Schrake, 7 B, Room 9, 253 North Noble street....................................	480
Carrie Cleaver, 6 B, Room 11, 327 East New York street...............................	530
Margaret Hamilton, Critic, 5 A and 5 B, Rooms 8 and 10, 102 Park avenue.........	800
Susie Bradley, 4 A, Room 12, 129 Peru street	530
Fannie Morrison, 4 B, Room 7, 331 North New Jersey street.........................	530
Anna D. Klinge, 3 A, Room 5, 305 East South street..................................	555
Augusta Franck, 3 B, Room 2, 154 North New Jersey street............................	505

Helen F. Bullard, 2 A, Room 3, 625 North Pennsylvania street............................	$505
Emily Tschirch, 2 B, Room 6, 333 Davidson street	555
Nettie Wolfram, 1 A, Room 13, 201 North New Jersey street............................	480
Rachel Segar, 1 B, Room 4, 227 East Washington street	530
Elnora Haag, German, Room 14, 31 Broadway..................................	530

No. 10.

Corner Home Avenue and Ash Street.

Henrie Colgan, Principal, 8 B, Room 6, 170 Christian avenue................................	1,000
Ruama Wales, 7 A, Room 10, 96 College avenue......................................	570
Amy E. Wales, 7 B, Room 8, 96 College avenue......................................	570
Marguerite Zearing, 6 A, Room 5, 233 College avenue.....................................	530
Rosa Dark, 5 A B, Room 9, 291 Broadway	530
Julia D. Ruick, 5 B, Room 7, 345 Ash street	530
Carrie Jones, 3 A, Room 12, 809 North Meridian street...................................	420
Ida Morse, 3 B, Room 11, 37 Ash street.........	480
Ella Norris, 2 A, Room 3, 231 Peru street.....	480
Ella Jones, 2 B, Room 1, 130 Ash street.......	480

Julia Ashley, 2 B and 1 A, Room 4, 158 Ash street...	$530
Lois Hoyt, 1 B, Room 2, 170 Rohampton street	530

University Building.

Mary H. Fulton, 6 B, Room 10, 444 North Tennessee street.................................	580
Lizzie Stearns, 6 B, Room 19, 288 Bellefontaine street...	450
Ida Nelson, 4 A, Room 11, 309 Ash street.....	450
Dute Lanham, 4 A B, Room 14, 124 Butler street...	530
Annie Morrison, 4 B, Room 12, 331 North New Jersey street...............................	530
Mary Dye, 3 B, Room 13, 178 Broadway	480

Brookside.

Kate Phipps, Grades 1, 2 and 3, 301 North Delaware street..	600

No. 11.

Corner Fourth and Tennessee Streets.

Emma Donnan, Principal, 8 B, Room 5, 126 North Tennessee street	950
Emily M. Ensign, 7 B, Room 7, 705 North Illinois street..	570
Laura Donnan, 6 B, Room 12, 126 North Tennessee street.....................................	530

Kate E. Espy, 5 B, Room 8, 526 North Illinois street	$530
Mattie Robinson, 4 A, Room 11, 876 North Mississippi street	480
Juliet Moore, 4 B, Room 10, 107 East St. Joseph street	530
Cora Day, 3 A, Room 3, 127 West Sixth street	480
Lizzie Meskill, 3 B, Room 2, 549 North Tennessee street	480
May Minich, 2 A, Room 1, 520 North Illinois street	480
May W. Donnan, 2 B, Room 4, 799 North Tennessee street	
Mary P. Currie, 1 A B, Room 6, 614 North Pennsylvania street	530
Emma Burwerth, German, (half day,) Room 9, 70 West Eighth street	240

No. 12.

Corner West and McCarty Streets.

Mary E. Perry, Principal, 6 B, Room 2, 132 West Vermont street	850
M. E. Cameron, 5 A B, Room 5, 318 Pleasant street	530
Emma Richman, 4 B, Room 7, 16 Fletcher avenue	400
Anna Swett, 3 A B, Room 6, 399 North Alabama street	480
Carrie McCormack, 3 B and 2 B, Room 8, 80 South Tennessee street	480

Laura Black, 2 B, Room 3, 85 Clifford avenue	$480
Dollie David, 1 A, Room 4, 210 Union street	400
Jennie S. Huron, 1 B, Room 1, 268 South Meridian street...............................	530
Marie Steffe, German, Room 9, 351 South Pennsylvania street...........................	530

No. 13.

Corner Buchanan and Beaty Streets.

M. S. Ingersoll, Principal, 8 B, Room 11, 165 East Merrill street................................	950
M. H. Ingersoll, 8 B, Room 10, 165 East Merrill street...	570
L. T. Benson, 7 B, Room 8, 16 East Michigan..	570
A. V. Demree, 6 A, Room 12, 305 East South street...	530
M. L. Mather, 6 B and 5 A, Room 9, 344 Olive street..	530
L. Van Deusen, 5 B, Room 7, 218 Huron street...	420
H. E. Galbraith, 4 A B, Room 3, 138 Massachusetts avenue..................................	530
N. A. Galbraith, 3 A, Room 4, 138 Massachusetts avenue.......................................	450
S. H. Harrison, 3 B, Room 5, 45 Huron street	480
Isabel King, Critic, 2 A. B, Rooms 1 and 2, 63 North East street...............................	700

N. J. Simpson, 1 A B, Room 6, 389 Virginia avenue..	$440
H. G. Sturm, German, 35 Coburn street..	530

No. 14.

Ohio Street, east of Highland Avenue.

Mary T. Lodge, Principal, 8 B and 7 B, Room 8, 732 East Washington street	850
Mary A. Hancock, 6 B, Room 6, 327 East New York street	530
Beatrice S. Foy, 5 B, Room 7, 90 Benton	530
Agnes C. Lannes, 4 A B, Room 2, 275 North Pine street	530
Millie S. Hancock, 3 B, Room 4, 327 East New York street	450
Dora Hall, 2 A B, Room 3, East Washington street	480
Mary Biedenmeister, 1 A B, Room 1, 265 East New York street	530
Louise Tschirch, German, 333 North Davidson street	450

No. 15.

Market Street, between West and California Streets.

Annie Barbour, Principal, 4 A B, Room 1, 216 North West street	700
Harrie G. Robinson, 3 A B, Room 3, 118 North Mississippi street	480
Lillian Gilmore, 2 A B, Room 4, 174 West Ohio street	400

PUBLIC SCHOOLS.

Myra H. Peck, 2 B, 1 A B, Room 2, 283 West Michigan street.................. $530

No. 16.

Indianola, corner Ray and Plum Streets.

M. V. Marshall, Principal, Grades 7, 6, 5, Room 2, 383 Massachusetts avenue........ 750
S. E. Prather, Grades 4, 3, Room 3, West Indianapolis 530
Bell Carroll, Grades 2, 1, Room 1, West Indianapolis 530

No. 17.

Corner Michigan Road and Huntington Street.

Jennie W. Bass, Principal, 5 B, Room 3, 318 North Delaware street..................... 700
Anna A. Courtney, 4 A B, Room 5, 325 Blake street... 420
Maggie M. Laird, 3 A B, Room 2, 454 North California street............................ 480
Prudie Lewis, 2 A B, Room 4, 325 North Mississippi street............................. 480
Ella Davis, 1 A B, Room 1, 590 North Illinois street 530

No. 18.

Yandes Street, between Home Avenue and Lincoln Street.

L. E. Christy, 8 B and 7 B, Room 1, 81 Yandes street.. 700

A. Harrison, 5 B and 4 B, Room 4, Excelsior
avenue.. $400
Elva H. Terry, 3 B and 2 B, Room 2, 28
Yandes street 480
Anna M. Spaulding, 1 A B, Room 3, 312 W.
Market street.. 480

No. 19.
Shelby Street, south of Prospect Street.

Mary R. Wilson, Principal, Grades 6, 5, 4,
Room 1, 240 Virginia avenue............... 750
Emily L. McCoy, Grades 3, 2, Room 2, 123
West South street.................................. 480
Sarah Youtsey, Grades 2, 1, Room 4, 169
Buchanan street 480

No. 20.
Spruce Street, south of Prospect Street.

Jennie Lindley, Principal, 6 A B, Room 2, 80
Peru street... 850
Auska Lindley, 5 A, Room 6, 80 Peru street... 530
Lucy Carle, 5 B and 4 A, Room 1, 32 School
street.. 530
Belle Lindley, 4 B, Room 7, 80 Peru street... 530
Fanny Murphy, 3 A, Room 8, 11 Smithson
street 400
Maria Trueman, 3 B, Reed street, Carlisle
Block 420
Florence Patterson, 2 A B, Room 5, 167 Prospect street... 480

Anna Wright, 2 B and 1 A, Room 4, 138 Massachusetts avenue	$530
Ida E. Anderson, 1, Room 3, 222 E. St. Clair street	480
Emma Grobe, German, Room 9, 276 South Meridian street	400

No. 21.

New York Street, between Illinois and Tennessee Streets.

Roxie Hall, Principal, 1 and 2, Room 4, 289 Bright street	450

No. 22.

Corner Chestnut and Hill Streets.

Mary A. McKeever, Principal, 6 B 5 A, Room 1, 342 South New Jersey street	850
Leonora Benson, 5 B 4 A, Room 8, 172 East Morris street	450
Mattie E. Rihl, 4 B, Room 7, 127 Lincoln street	400
Alfie C. Wilmot, 3 B, Room 3, 373 Coburn street	480
Lydia B. Morris, 2 A B, Room 4, 156 North Illinois street	480
Mary A. Calhoun, 1 A B, Room 2, 795 North Tennessee street	530
Minna Ebmeier, German, Room 6, 314 Union street	530

No. 23.

Corner Fourth and Howard Streets.

Ben. D. Bagby, Principal, 6 B and 5 B, Room 1, 289 Blake street...............................	$700
K. C. Evans, 4 B and 3 B, Room 4, 758 North Tennessee street....................................	480
S. A. McCary, 3 A and 2 A B, Room 3, 217 West Michigan street................................	480
E. V. Gentry, 1 A B, Room 2, 641 North Mississippi street..	420

No. 24.

Corner North and Minerva Streets.

Robert B. Bagby, Principal, 8 B and 7 B, Room 3, 289 Blake street...............................	850
Saidie V. W. Ireland, 6 B, Room 7............	530
Wm. D. McCoy, 5 B, Room 8, 79 Kentucky avenue..	480
Mary E. Willson, 4 B, Room 6, 480 West North street..	480
Victoria A. Willson, 3 B, Room 5, 480 West North street..	480
Mary G. Carter, 2 B, Room 1, 480 W. North street..	480
H. C. Campbell, 1 B, Room 4, corner State and Sturm streets..................................	530

No. 25.

Corner New Jersey and Merrill Streets.

Etta Bradshaw, Principal, 6 B and 5 A, Room 3, 196 South New Jersey street.............	$850
N. Van de Grift, 5 B, Room 8, 306 South Meridian street......................................	530
M. E. Ware, 4 A B, Room 6, 178 Broadway..	530
Maie C. LeMonde, 3 A, Room 5, near Crown Hill...	400
M. Haslep, 3 B, Room 7, 255 Virginia avenue Augusta M. Siddall, 2 A, Room 4, 227 East Louisiana street...................................	480
Jesse B. Miller, 2 B, Room 2, 266 South Meridian street	400
Lottie Homan, 1 A B, Room 1, 154 S. New Jersey street.......................................	420
Laura Grobe, German, Room 9, 276 South Meridian street	450

Boundaries of Districts

FOR SCHOOL PURPOSES.

The following boundaries designate the districts for school purposes, and the number and location of the school houses in each district, both for Grammar and Primary schools.

Pupils must attend the school in the district in which they reside. This rule is imperative unless for some special reason the superintendent of schools transfers pupils to another district.

No. 1.
Corner Vermont and New Jersey Streets.

PRIMARY.

Beginning at the intersection of Michigan and Liberty streets; thence south by the center of Liberty to the Union Railway; thence along the Union railway to Delaware street; thence north by the center of Delaware street to Virginia avenue; thence by the center of Virginia avenue to Washington street; thence east by the center of Washington street to Delaware street; thence north by the center of Delaware street to Michigan street; thence east by the center of Michigan street to Liberty street.

No. 2.

Corner Delaware and Walnut Streets.

PRIMARY AND GRAMMAR.

Beginning at the intersection of Liberty and Michigan streets; thence west by the center of Michigan street to Illinois street; thence north by the center of Illinois street to First street; thence east by the center of First street to Pennsylvania street; thence north by the center of Pennsylvania street to Home avenue; thence east to Central avenue; thence south by the center of Central avenue to Cherry street; thence east by the center of Cherry street to Park avenue; thence south by the center of Park avenue and Liberty street to Michigan street.

No. 3.

Meridian Street, between Ohio and New York Streets.

GRAMMAR.

Commencing at the intersection of Michigan and East streets; thence south by the center of East street to the Union railway tracks; thence west along said tracks to Missouri street; thence north by the center of Missouri street to North street; thence East by the center of North street to Illinois street; thence south by the center of Illinois street to Michigan street;

thence east by the center of Michigan street to East street the place of beginning.

PRIMARY.

Beginning at the intersection of Michigan and Delaware streets; thence south by the center of Delaware street to Washington street; thence west to Missouri street. Western and northern boundaries the same as above.

No. 4.

Corner of Michigan and Blackford Streets.

GRAMMAR.

Beginning at the intersection of First street and Lafayette railroad; thence south by Lafayette railroad tracks to the Union railway tracks; thence along said railway tracks to White river; thence northward along White river to First street; thence east on First street to the Lafayette railroad, the place of beginning.

PRIMARY.

For primary purposes the southern boundary in the center of New York street, and the northern boundary is the center of North street and Indiana avenue.

No. 5.

Maryland Street, between Mississippi and Missouri Streets.

PRIMARY.

Beginning at the intersection of Pennsylvania and Washington streets; thence by the center of Virginia

SCHOOL PURPOSES. 71

avenue to Delaware street; thence south by the center of Delaware street to the Union railway tracks; thence along said tracks to White river; thence north along said river to Washington street; thence east by the center of Washington street to the place of beginning.

No. 6.
Corner Union and Phipps Streets.

GRAMMAR AND PRIMARY.

Beginning at the intersection of the Union railway tracks and the J., M. and I. R. R.; thence south by the J. M. & I. R. R. to the center of Ray street; thence west along the center of Ray street to Tennessee street; thence north by the center of Tennessee street to the Union railway tracks; thence east by the Union railway tracks to the place of beginning.

No. 7.
Corner of Bates and Benton Streets.

PRIMARY AND GRAMMAR.

Beginning at the intersection of the corporation line and Michigan road; thence by the center of Michigan road to Washington street; thence west by the center of Washington street to the C., C., C. & I. R. R.; thence along said railway to Virginia avenue; thence south on Virginia avenue to Louisiana street; thence east by the center of Louisiana street to East street; thence south by the center of East street to

South street; thence east by the center of South street and Fletcher avenue to corporation line; thence north on corporation line to the place of beginning.

No. 8.
Virginia Avenue, corner Huron Street.
PRIMARY.

Beginning at the intersection of Virginia avenue and South street; thence east along the center of South street and Fletcher avenue to Dillon street; thence south by the center of Dillon street to Virginia avenue; thence northwest by the center of Virginia avenue to McCarty street; thence west by the center of McCarty street to East street; thence north by the center of East street to the place of beginning.

No. 9.
Corner Vermont and Davidson Streets.
GRAMMAR.

Beginning at the intersection of East and Michigan streets; thence south by the center of East street to the C., C., C. & I. R. R. track; thence northeast along said track to St. Clair street; thence west by the center of St. Clair street to Liberty street; thence south by the center of Liberty street to Michigan street; thence west by the center of Michigan street to the place of beginning.

PRIMARY.

The western boundary is the center of Liberty street.

No. 10.

Corner Home Avenue and Ash Street.

PRIMARY AND GRAMMAR.

Beginning at the intersection of St. Clair street and Park avenue; thence east by the center of St. Clair street to Pogue's Run; thence north by Pogue's Run to Clifford avenue; thence north by the east corporation line to the north corporation line; thence west by the north corporation line to Alabama street; thence south by the center of Alabama street to Home avenue; thence east by the center of Home avenue to Central avenue; thence south by the center of Central avenue to Cherry street; thence east by the center of Cherry street to Park avenue; thence south by the center of Park avenue to the place of beginning.

No. 11.

Corner Fourth and Tennessee Streets.

GRAMMAR.

Beginning at the intersection of North street and the Canal; thence east by the center of North street to Illinois street; thence north by the center of Illinois street to First street; thence east by the center of First street to Pennsylvania street; thence north by the center of Pennsylvania street to Home avenue; thence east by the center of Home avenue to Alabama street; thence north by the center of

Alabama street to the corporation line; thence west by the north corporation line to the west corporation line; thence south by the west corporation line to the line of First street; thence east by the center of First street to the Canal; thence south by the Canal to the place of beginning.

PRIMARY.

For primary schools, the west boundary is the Canal.

No. 12.

Corner West and McCarty Streets.

PRIMARY AND GRAMMAR.

Beginning at the intersection of White river and the T. H. & I. R. R ; thence east along said R. R. to Tennessee street; thence south by the center of Tennessee street and the line of Tennessee street to the corporation line; thence west by the corporation line to White river; thence along White river to the place of beginning.

No. 13.

Corner Buchanan and Beaty Streets.

GRAMMAR.

Beginning at the intersection of East and South streets; thence east by the center of South street and Fletcher avenue to Dillon street; thence south by the center of Dillon and Shelby streets to the corporation line; thence west to East street; thence north by the center of East street to the place of beginning.

PRIMARY.

For primary schools, the northern boundary is the center of McCarty street and Virginia avenue.

No. 14.

Ohio Street, east of Highland Avenue.

PRIMARY AND GRAMMAR.

Beginning at the intersection of Washington street and the Union railway tracks; thence east by the center of Washington street to the Michigan road; thence south-east by the center of Michigan road to State street; thence north by the center of State street to Washington street; thence east by the center of Washington street to the city limits; thence north on the east line of the city to Clifford avenue; thence west by the center of Clifford avenue to Pogue's Run; thence south by Pogue's Run to St. Clair street; thence west by the center of St. Clair street to the C., C., C & I. railway tracks; thence southward along the railway tracks to place of beginning.

No. 15.

Market Street, between West and California Streets.

PRIMARY.

Beginning at the intersection of New York street and the Lafayette railroad; thence south along the

Lafayette railroad to Washington street; thence west by the center of Washington street to White river; thence north along White river and the mill-race to New York street; thence east by the center of New York street to the place of beginning.

No. 16.
Indianola, corner Ray and Plum Streets.

PRIMARY AND GRAMMAR.

No. 16 includes all territory within the city limits west of White river.

No. 17.
Corner West Michigan Road and Huntington Street.

PRIMARY.

Beginning at the intersection of North street and the Canal; thence west by the center of North street to Indiana avenue; thence west by the center of Indiana avenue to the corporation line; thence east by the corporation line to the Canal; thence south by the Canal to the place of beginning.

No. 18.
Yandes Street, between Home Avenue and Lincoln Street.

No. 19.
Shelby Street, south of Prospect Street.

Nos. 18 and 19 are schools for colored pupils, with no boundaries prescribed.

No. 20.

Spruce Street, south of Prospect Street.

PRIMARY AND GRAMMAR.

Beginning at the intersection of Shelby street and the corporation line; thence east to the east corporation line; thence north by the east corporation line to the line of Fletcher avenue; thence east by the center of Fletcher avenue to Dillon street; thence south by the center of Dillon street and Shelby street to the place of beginning.

No. 21.

New York Street, between Illinois and Tennessee Streets.

School for colored pupils. No boundaries prescribed.

No. 22.

Corner Chestnut and Hill Streets.

PRIMARY AND GRAMMAR.

Beginning at the intersection of Ray and Tennessee streets; thence east by the center of Ray street to the J., M. & I. R. R.; thence south on the J., M. & I. R. R. to the line of Coburn street; thence east by the center of Coburn street to the intersection of Coburn street and the first alley east of High street; thence south by the center of said alley to Yeiser street; thence east by the center of Yeiser street to East street; thence south by the center of East street to the corporation line; thence west by the corporation line to Tennessee street; thence north on Tennessee street to Ray street the place of beginning.

No. 23.

Corner Fourth and Howard Streets.

No. 24.

Corner North and Minerva Streets.

Nos. 23 and 24 are schools for colored pupils, with no boundaries prescribed.

No. 25.

Corner New Jersey and Merrill Streets.

PRIMARY AND GRAMMAR.

Beginning at the junction of the Union railway tracks and the J., M. & I. R. R; thence south by the J., M. & I. R. R. to line of Coburn street; thence east by the center of Coburn street to the intersection of Coburn street and the first alley east of High street; thence south by the center of said alley to Yeiser street; thence east by the center of Yeiser street to East street; thence north by the center of East street to Louisiana street; thence west by the center of Louisiana street to Virginia avenue; thence northwest by the center of Virginia avenue to the Union railway tracks; thence west along the Union railway tracks to the place of beginning.

Rules and Regulations

FOR THE

GOVERNMENT

OF THE

Public Schools of Indianapolis

CLASSIFICATION.

The Public Schools of the city shall be divided into twelve grades. The four lowest grades shall constitute the Primary Department, the second four grades the Grammar Department, and the four highest grades the High School Department.

The District Schools comprise the Primary and Grammar Departments.

TERMS, VACATIONS, HOLIDAYS, ETC.

SECTION 1. The school year shall consist of ten months of four weeks each, and shall commence on the first Monday of September of each year. Thanksgiving day and the day following, and the twenty-second day of February shall be observed as holidays. The schools may be closed by order of the Board upon other days, not to exceed three days in the school year.

SEC. 2. There shall be three vacations each year as follows: One during the Christmas holidays, the duration of which shall be determined each year by the Board of School Commissioners; one of a week's duration, commencing on the last Monday in March, and one of ten weeks' duration in the months of June, July and August. The President of the Board may grant leave of absence from school to any teacher for a satisfactory reason.

SCHOOL HOURS.

SEC. 3. HIGH SCHOOL.—The daily session of the High School begins at 8:40 A. M., and closes at 1:30 P. M.

TRAINING SCHOOL.—The daily session of the Training School begins at 8:30 A. M., and closes at 1:00 P. M.

DISTRICT SCHOOLS —The morning session of the District Schools begins at 9 A. M., and closes at 12 M. The afternoon session begins at 1:30 P. M., and closes at 3:30 P. M , for second and third grades, and for all other grades at 4 P. M.

ASSISTANT SUPERINTENDENTS AND THEIR DUTIES.

SEC. 4. The Assistant Superintendents shall be responsible, under the direction of the Superintendent, for the observance and enforcement of the Rules and Regulations of the Board of School Commissioners, and in the discharge of these duties shall be entitled to the respect and deference of the teachers. They shall visit all the schools as often as practicable; pay particular attention to the classification of the pupils in the several schools, and to the apportionment among the classes of the prescribed studies. They shall be authorized, at any time during the year, to promote any pupil to a grade higher than the one to which he belongs, or to send him to the grade next below, as they may think the best interests of the pupil and the school require. In passing daily from school to school they shall endeavor to transfer improvements and remedy defects.

SEC. 5. The Assistant Superintendents shall make monthly reports to the Superintendent of the number of visits made by them respectively to the several schools under their supervision, together with a statement of the amount of time spent in each school. It shall also be their duty immediately after the semi-annual and annual examinations of each year to make a careful report to him of the work, methods of instruction employed, and success of each one of the teachers, together with any suggestions they may have to make respecting the course of study, discipline, or other topics of general interest, and to co operate with the Superintendent in carrying out the directions of the Board.

PRINCIPAL OF NORMAL SCHOOL.

SEC. 6. It shall be the duty of the Principal of the Normal School to investigate as carefully as possible the moral character of all candidates for entrance to his school; to direct the examinations for entrance, and, under the direction of the Superintendent, to decide upon the admission of all pupils. He shall direct the methods of instruction employed in the Normal School, and plan the course of study pursued by the pupil-teachers. He shall have such general oversight of the practice-schools as shall tend to the realization in these schools of the methods taught in the theory department.

SEC. 7. It shall be the duty of the several critic teachers to plan in detail the daily work of the pupil-teachers assigned to their charge, and assist these teachers in carrying out the same with the pupils. They shall frequently talk over in a kindly way with their practice-teachers, the successes and failures in the daily work of the latter, devising means of removing defects and increasing efficiency in such work. The critics shall so supplement the work of practice-teachers that the schools taught by them shall not materially suffer from the inexperience of such practice-teachers. They shall report to the Principal of the Normal School, from time to time, the degree of proficiency attained by each practice-teacher under their charge, together with any suggestion tending to increase such proficiency. They shall attend any meetings called by the Principal of the Normal School for discussion of methods of instruction or discipline, or for the consideration of any topic pertaining to the management of the practice-schools.

SUPERVISING SPECIAL TEACHERS.

Sec. 8. It shall be the duty of the Supervising Special Teachers to plan as definitely as may be the work in their respective subjects, and visit as often as practicable the various school-rooms of the city, either instructing the pupils or examining them with a view to determine the efficiency of the instruction given by the regular teacher in charge. They shall make a written report to the Superintendent, annually, and at such other times as he may direct, showing the methods of instruction employed, and the condition and progress of the work in their respective subjects, together with such suggestions and recommendations as will in their opinion remedy existing defects or increase the efficiency of the work in their departments. They shall give such instruction in the Saturday Institutes as will give to the regular teacher of each school an intelligent comprehension of the work to be done by her in these subjects between the visits of the Special Teacher.

Sec. 9. Each Special Teacher shall work upon a regular programme, arranged by him under the direction of the Superintendent.

PRINCIPALS.

Sec. 10. Principals shall be held responsible for the general management of their several schools. They shall see that the school-houses are opened at 8:15 A. M., and the hour announced by the ringing of the bells on all the school-houses that have them. The rooms shall be made comfortably warm at this hour, and the Principal, with one or more teachers, shall be present and exercise a general care over the pupils, and at all times they shall give special attention to the protection, health and comfort of the pupils. They shall punctually observe the hours for opening and closing schools. They shall establish special rules for securing good order in the stairways, halls and school-yards under their supervision, and for preventing pupils from collecting in groups in the adjacent streets and alleys before and after school.

Sec. 11. They shall see that the school buildings are properly cleaned, warmed and ventilated, and shall be held responsible for any want of neatness or cleanliness about the school premises, and they shall prescribe such rules for the use of the outbuildings connected with the school-houses as shall insure their being kept in a neat and proper condition. It shall be the duty of the Principal of each school to cause the doors of the coal-houses and the outside doors of his school-house to be locked and the windows and window-shutters of the same to be properly closed every day after the close of school.

SEC. 12. They shall examine the registers of the teachers as often as once a month, and give such direction and assistance as may be necessary to secure accuracy and uniformity.

SEC. 13. They shall see that the teachers within their respective buildings are promptly notified and duly advised as to all rules and regulations pertaining to the government and classification of their schools, and that they carry out the same in every particular. They shall see that parents are duly notified of the absence of their children in all cases when the cause of absence is unknown, or is not satisfactory to the teacher; and they shall have power to suspend pupils temporarily for insubordination or irregularity of attendance.

SEC. 14. They shall report to the Superintendent upon the Tuesday succeeding the close of each school month, the condition of their several schools, and shall make an annual report at the close of the year in accordance with the requirements, upon blanks furnished for the purpose, and shall report to the Superintendent any refusal, after due and proper admonition, on the part of a teacher or pupil to comply with the regulations of the Board.

TEACHERS.

SEC. 15. No person under the age of nineteen years shall be appointed as teacher in any public school.

Sec. 16. Teachers who pass the examination required by the Board shall receive a trial certificate, testifying to their moral character and intellectual attainments. At the expiration of the time for which the trial certificate was granted they shall be granted a permanent certificate; *Provided*, They shall sustain a satisfactory examination in the additional branches required by the Board; and *Provided, further*, That their services in instruction and discipline have been satisfactory to the Committee on Appointment of Teachers and to the Superintendent.

Sec. 17. The tenure of office of all teachers shall be at the pleasure of the Board, and superior qualifications as to moral character, literary attainments, industry and practical skill shall be specially regarded in their employment and continuance.

They shall have the right to resign only when two weeks' notice of such intention is given, and the Board reserves the right to suspend or dismiss any teacher, for violation of rules, unfitness or incompetence, at any time.

Sec. 18. Whenever any teacher shall be temporarily absent from school, it shall be the duty of the said teacher to send notice forthwith to the Principal of the school, with a statement of the reason and probable time of such absence, and if any doubt exists in respect to the time of returning, then the teacher shall afterwards send seasonable notice to the Principal of the school of the time when she is to return. When a teacher returns to school after a temporary absence and fails to send notice, as required above, in time to save the substitute the trouble of going to the school, the substitute shall receive pay for one half-day, and the same shall be deducted from the pay of the teacher. All teachers when absent from school shall forfeit their salaries during the continuance of such absence.

In case of the absence of a Principal, the notices above required shall be sent to the Superintendent.

SEC. 19. Substitutes for teachers absent shall be employed by the Principals, under the direction of the Superintendent, at such compensation as may be fixed by the Board.

SEC. 20. All teachers shall devote themselves exclusively to the duties of their schools during school hours, and shall use every available means for their improvement in the work of instruction and discipline. They shall attend faithfully such meetings as may be called by the Superintendent for counsel and mutual improvement; and for absence from, or tardiness at, such meeting, shall suffer the same deduction from their salaries as herein provided for absence or tardiness in their daily work.

SEC. 21. They shall make a faithful record upon the daily register of all items required therein, and shall make, before leaving the school-building, upon the last Friday of each school month, an accurate monthly report to the Principal, in accordance with instructions on monthly report blanks. They shall keep such other records, and make such other reports, as the Superintendent may require. All work except the daily record must be done outside of school hours.

Sec. 22. All the teachers are expected to make themselves familiar with the provisions of these regulations, and to co-operate with the Board at all times in taking such measures as may be necessary to secure their observance. A faithful compliance with all rules relating to teachers shall be one of the conditions on which they retain their connection with the Public Schools.

Sec. 23. All the teachers of the Public Schools are required to be at their respective school rooms and report themselves to the Principal, both morning and afternoon, at least fifteen minutes before the hour of opening schools, and all teachers failing to report, except from sickness or unavoidable cause, shall suffer a deduction from their salaries of one-fourth of a day's pay for each failure.

All teachers are expected to enter upon the opening services of their respective schools at the precise minute appointed, and on no account shall they dismiss their pupils earlier than the appointed time, nor for any day or part of a day, without permission from the Superintendent.

Sec. 24. The morning exercises in each school shall commence with reading the scriptures or other appropriate matter, and that exercise may be followed by the repetition of the Lord's Prayer and by appropriate singing.

All teachers shall carefully guard against the introduction of questions of a sectarian or partisan character. They shall also refuse to read or to circulate any advertisement of any kind whatever, and shall not allow any person the privilege of exhibiting any book, map or other articles, or of reading or announcing, in any form, any advertisement or notice of any entertainment, or of distributing upon school premises any books, tracts or other publications. They shall not receive any present obtained by contributions from the pupils. No teacher shall allow a subscription or contribution of any kind to be taken up in any Public School without the consent of the Board.

Sec 25. Each teacher shall be held responsible for the order and discipline of his own room, practicing such discipline as would be exercised by a kind, firm and judicious parent in his family.

Sec. 26. They shall avoid corporal punishment when good discipline can be preserved by milder means.

Each teacher shall make out a full and complete statement in writing of each case in which corporal punishment has been inflicted by him upon any pupil, specifying the name, age and grade of the pupil punished, the offense charged, and the kind and degree of punishment inflicted, which statement shall be given to the Principal, to be by him forwarded immediately to the Superintendent.

Sec. 27. The teachers of all grades in the District Schools shall allow a recess each half day, not exceeding fifteen minutes from the time the pupils leave their seats until they are again seated. Whenever pupils are detained in the school-room at recess, they shall be allowed to pass out after the recess is closed. All pupils shall be required to pass out of the school-room at recess, unless it would occasion an exposure of health; but they shall never be required to remain out when the exposure would be injurious to health.

The teachers in the Public Schools are not permitted to detain any pupil at the noon recess for any purpose other than that of discipline, and the detention for this cause shall be determined upon by the teacher and Principal of the building.

Teachers may detain pupils at the close of the afternoon session for purposes of discipline, instruction or study, not to exceed thirty minutes, provided that pupils in the primary grades shall not be detained for study.

Sec. 28. Teachers shall have charge of such classes as may be assigned them by the Committee on Appointment of Teachers and the Superintendent. They shall be subject to the direction of the Principals, and shall co-operate with them not only during school hours but during the time when the pupils are on the school premises, before and after school and during recesses.

Sec. 29. Teachers shall be permitted to visit other schools of the same grade as their own, for purposes of improvement, not exceeding in all two half-days in any one year, and their schools shall be dismissed during the time of such visits.

When teachers are thus permitted to visit other schools they shall spend the entire time of the school session in observing the work of such teachers as the Superintendent or his Assistants may designate.

Sec. 30. No teacher shall be allowed to employ his time outside of school hours in any manner which will, in the Opinion of the Committee upon the Appointment of Teachers, interfere with his efficiency or usefulness as a teacher in the Public Schools.

Sec. 31. It shall be the duty of each teacher to read to the pupils, from time to time, so much of the rules as apply to them, that they may have a clear understanding of the rules by which they are governed.

VENTILATION AND TEMPERATURE.

Sec. 32. It shall be the duty of the teachers to give vigilant attention to the ventilation and temperature of their school rooms, and to make themselves familiar with the means by which their respective rooms may be properly ventilated. A regular system of ventilation shall be practiced in winter as well as in summer, by which the air in all their school rooms shall be effectually changed at recess, and at such other times as may be necessary to prevent the breathing of impure air. Children shall in no case be allowed to sit in a draught of air.

Sec. 33 —None but the children and wards of bona fide residents of Indianapolis and those properly transferred in accordance with the school law shall be admitted to the Public Schools, and none shall be admitted who are not at least six years of age, *Provided*, That the Superintendent may admit pupils who are non-residents on payment of tuition at the rate of twenty-five dollars per year for each pupil in the district schools, and forty dollars for each pupil in the High School in case such admission will not prevent the seating of resident pupils.

MEMBERSHIP OF PUPILS.

Sec. 34. Pupils must attend the school in the district in which they reside; unless for some special reason the Superintendent of Schools transfers pupils to another district.

Sec. 35. No pupil shall be admitted into any public school who cannot furnish satisfactory evidence that he or she has been vaccinated or otherwise secured against smallpox, and no pupil affected with any contagious disease, or coming from a house where such disease exists, shall be allowed to remain in any public school.

Sec. 36. Any child coming to school without proper attention having been given to the cleanliness of his person or his dress, or whose clothes need repairing, may be sent home to be properly prepared for the school room.

Sec. 37. No pupil shall be allowed to retain connection with any public school unless furnished with books, slate and other articles required: *Provided,* That no pupil shall be excluded for such cause until the parent or guardian shall have had one week's notice, and been furnished by the teacher with a list of the books or articles needed

Sec. 38. Whenever a pupil passes from one public school to another, he shall be required to present to the Principal of the school which he wishes to enter, a certificate from the Principal of the school which he leaves, stating that he is in good standing at the time of leaving, and specifying the grade and class to which he belongs. He shall then be allowed to enter a class in the same grade as that which he left.

Sec. 39. In all cases of absence from school, whether with intention of returning or not, whether the absence be occasioned by sickness or other causes including suspension of pupils; but excepting solely the case of transfer to some other public school in this city, the pupil's name shall be kept on the roll as belonging for three days and dropped uniformly in case he does not return at the beginning of the seventh half day.

ATTENDANCE OF PUPILS.

Sec. 40. In all cases of tardiness or absence, excuses shall be required of parents or guardians, in writing or in person, stating the cause of the same. When such an excuse is not sent by the pupil, the teacher may send for it, with permission of principal. Excuses shall be valid only in case of sickness of pupil, family, or other urgent necessity.

Any pupil in the High School or in the Grammar Department who shall be absent four half-days in four consecutive weeks, without valid excuse; also, any pupil in the Primary Department who shall be absent six half-days in the same length of time, without like excuse, shall be suspended from attendance at the school, such suspension to remain in force until satisfactory assurance is given that attendance will, as far as possible, be regular thereafter.

In every case of unexcused absence, the teacher shall inform the parent or guardian, either in person or by note, as early as practicable.

In the application of the foregoing rule, *each tardiness* shall be regarded as *an absence.*

Absences which occur when the attendance of the pupil would occasion a serious and imprudent exposure of health, shall be regarded the same as absences occasioned by sickness.

Whenever the absence of the pupil is occasioned by sickness and the teacher does not receive a proper notice of the cause till the pupil is suspended, the pupil should be restored upon an explanation of the cause, either in person or by note to the teacher and not to the Superintendent.

DUTIES OF PUPILS.

SEC. 41. All pupils shall be cleanly in person

and dress, polite in conduct, truthful and chaste in language, and studious during school-hours.

The use of tobacco and of profane language upon or about the school premises is strictly forbidden.

Pupils shall be quiet and respectful on the streets and about the school premises. They shall not mar nor deface nor injure, in any manner whatever, the desks or furniture of the school-rooms, the walls or ceilings of the school buildings, the stairways, fences or outbuildings upon the school grounds.

Any damage done to school property by any pupil, shall be repaired at the expense of the party committing the trespass.

Pupils shall be held responsible for their conduct on their way to and from school.

SEC. 42. For violation of any of the provisions of this section the pupil may be suspended by the teacher, with the concurrence of the Principal, in which case the teacher shall immediately report such suspension, with a written statement of the reason thereof, to the parent or guardian and to the Superintendent.

SEC. 43. Whenever the Principal of any school shall report to the Superintendent the name of any pupil whose conduct is considered such, in school or out, that he is unfit to be a member of the school, the Superintendent shall examine the case without delay, and if in his opinion the pupil has been duly admonished, and reformation appears to be hopeless, he may suspend such pupil from school.

RESTORATION OF PUPILS.

SEC. 44. In case of suspension for absence or tardiness under the provisions of section 40, the pupil may be restored on a first suspension by the Principal; but on a second or subsequent suspension he shall be restored by the Superintendent only.

Pupils suspended for any cause other than absence or tardiness shall be restored by the Superintendent only.

SEC. 45. No lessons for home study shall be assigned to pupils of primary grades.

To pupils of grades five and six may be assigned one lesson, only, and to pupils of grades seven and eight may be assigned two lessons one of which shall be spelling.

Pupils studying German may be required, in addition to the home study above provided for, to prepare at home any lesson prepared by other pupils during the time devoted to German upon the daily programme.

SEC. 46. There shall be a written examination for the promotion of pupils, held at the middle and at the close of each school year.

INSTRUCTION IN GERMAN.

SEC. 47. Instruction in the German language shall be given in the second, third, fourth, sixth, seventh, ninth, eleventh, twelveth, thirteenth fourteenth, twentieth, twenty second and twenty-fifth districts, and in the High School.

SEC. 48. Hereafter instruction in German shall be introduced into such schools as have an attendance of one hundred or more pupils who wish to study German, provided the school be held in a building suitable for the purpose, and that the parents of the children attending the school shall petition therefor.

SEC. 49. There shall be appointed a Teacher of German for the High School, who shall also be Supervisor of German Instruction in the District Schools. He shall devise such plans as may be expedient or necessary, and report semi-annually to the Superintendent the condition of said classes. He shall furnish the different German Teachers with instruction respecting the lessons and books, and is empowered to convene them at some convenient time to consult with them about the best methods, and other matters pertaining to his department. He shall visit at least one school each day, without neglecting his classes; he shall examine the different schools and classes at the end of every scholastic year independent of the German examination, and in general be governed by the corresponding rules and regulations of the Board applicable to him, as teacher and officer.

SEC. 50. Female teachers shall be employed, if they can be obtained; but no teacher shall be deemed competent to instruct in the German Department unless proficient also in English.

SEC. 51. Instruction in German shall commence in the second grade.

Sec. 52. The recitations of German classes are to be as follows: In the second grade two lessons per day, one in the forenoon of twenty minutes and one in the afternoon of fifteen minutes. In grades three to eight inclusive one lesson of thirty minutes each day.

Sec. 53. The instruction in the German language must adapt itself to the English classes, and the above rules as to time shall be subject to the necessities of the general programme.

Sec. 54. Pupils studying German shall be allowed one-half the time devoted to writing in school for the purpose of practicing German script, provided the German teacher can arrange to supervise the same.

The German language is to be used in giving instruction so far as it can be understood by the pupils.

Sec. 55. Whenever it is practicable, the instruction in English should be so regulated by the Principals of the different schools as not to overburden the pupils who wish to learn German.

Sec. 56. No pupil who has entered a German class shall leave the same without the most urgent reasons, to be judged by the Superintendent.

Sec. 57. The classes in German shall be formed at the beginning of the school year, and no pupils shall be admitted to them later, except after due examination and approval by the Supervisor of German.

Sec. 58. The boundaries of the several schools in which German is taught shall be no hindrance to a pupil who, residing in a district in which German is not taught, wishes to join a German class.

MISCELLANEOUS.

Sec. 59. Whenever a parent or guardian wishes his child to pursue a partial course of study, or to leave school during school hours at stated times, the Superintendent may grant such permission; *Provided*, There are good reasons for the same, and the interests of the school will not be seriously interfered with.

Sec. 60. No Principal, teacher or janitor in any of the Public Schools of this city, nor any other employe of this Board shall sell, or keep for sale, or in any manner act as agent for the sale of any book, map, card, paper, pencil, rubber or any other material used in any of the Public Schools.

Sec. 61. The school-buildings under the control of the Board of School Commissioners shall not be used for any other purpose than the accommodation of the Public Schools, except by a special vote of the Board.

Sec. 62. The foregoing Rules are adopted as a Revised Code of Rules, and all rules adopted prior to this revision are hereby rescinded.

TIME TABLES.

The following time tables are suggested for the work in the several grades, but they are subject to any modification desired by individual teachers, provided, (1) that the relative amount of time per week therein prescribed for each subject shall not be materially changed, and (2) that a copy of every revised programme shall be submitted to the Superintendent. The latter provision is essential because the programmes are arranged partly for the convenience of supervisors.

PROGRAMMES.

FIRST GRADE.

Advanced Class.

A. M.

9:00 to 9:10 Opening exercises.
9:10 to 9:25 Reading and spelling, Class 3.
9:25 to 9:40 Reading and spelling, Class 2.
9:40 to 9:50 Number, Class 1
9:50 to 10:05 General lesson.

10:05 to 10:15 Number, Class 3.
10:15 to 10:30 Reading, Class 2.
10:30 to 10:45 Recess.
10:45 to 11:00 Reading, Class 1.
11:00 to 11:10 Number, Class 2.
11:10 to 11:20 Reading, Class 3.
11:20 to 11:35 Writing.
11:35 to 11:50 Reading, Class 1.
11:50 to 12:00 Music.

Beginning Class.

P. M.

1:30 to 1:40 Opening exercises.
1:40 to 1:50 Reading and spelling, Class 2.
1:50 to 2:00 Number, Class 1.
2:00 to 2:10 Reading and spelling, Class 3.
2:10 to 2:20 Number, Class 2.
2:20 to 2:35 General lesson.
2:35 to 2:45 Reading and spelling, Class 1.
2:45 to 3:00 Recess.
3:00 to 3:15 Writing.
3:15 to 3:25 Reading and spelling, Class 3.
3:25 to 3:35 Reading and spelling, Class 2.
3:35 to 3:50 Reading and spelling, Class 1.
3:50 to 4:00 Music.

SECOND GRADE.

A. M.

9:00 to 9:10 Opening exercises.
9:10 to 9:20 Spelling (oral), Class 1.

9:20 to 9:40 Reading, Class 2.
9:40 to 10:00 Number, Class 1.
10:00 to 10:10 Spelling (oral), Class 2.
10:10 to 10:30 General lesson.
10:30 to 10:45 Recess.
10:45 to 11:05 Reading, Class 1.
11:05 to 11:25 Writing.
11:25 to 11:40 Number, Class 2.
11:40 to 11:50 Spelling (written), Classes 1 and 2.
11:50 to 12:00 Music.

P. M.

1:30 to 1:55 Reading and spelling, Class 2.
1:55 to 2:10 Number, Class 1.
2:10 to 2:25 Drawing.
2:25 to 2:45 Number, Class 2.
2:45 to 3:00 Recess.
3:00 to 3:20 Reading, Class 1.
3:20 to 3:30 Music.

THIRD GRADE.

A. M.

9:00 to 9:10 Opening exercises.
9:10 to 9:30 Number, Class 2.
9:30 to 9:50 Reading, Class 1.
9:50 to 10:10 Writing.
10:10 to 10:30 General lesson.
10:30 to 10:45 Recess.
10:45 to 10:55 Spelling (oral).
10:55 to 11:15 Reading, Class 2.

11:15 to 11:35 Number, Class 1.
11:35 to 11:45 Written spelling.
11:45 to 12:00 Music.

P. M.

1:30 to 1:55 Reading and spelling, Class 2.
1:55 to 2:10 Number, Class 1.
2:10 to 2:25 Drawing.
2:25 to 2:45 Number, Class 2.
2:45 to 3:00 Recess.
3:00 to 3:20 Reading and spelling, Class 1.
3:20 to 3:30 Music.

FOURTH GRADE.

A. M.

	RECITATIONS.	STUDY.
9:00 to 9:10	Opening exercises.	
9:10 to 9:40	Arithmetic, Class 1.	Arith , Class 2.
9:40 to 10:10	Arithmetic Class 2.	Geog., Class 1.
10:10 to 10:30	Drawing.	
10:30 to 10:45	Recess.	
10:45 to 11:10	Reading, Class 1.	Rd. or lg., Cl. 2.
11:10 to 11:35	Reading, Class 2.	Rd. or lg., Cl. 1.
11:35 to 12:00	Writing.	

P. M.

1:30 to 1:55	Language, Class 1.	Geog , Class 2.
1:55 to 2:20	Language, Class 2.	Arith., Class 1.
2:20 to 2:45	Geography, Class 1.	Arith., Class 2.
2:45 to 3:00	Recess.	

	RECITATIONS.	STUDY.

3:00 to 3:25 Geography, Class 2. Arith., Class 1.
3:25 to 3:40 Spelling.
3:40 to 4:00 Music.

FIFTH GRADE.
A. M.

	RECITATIONS.	STUDY.

9:00 to 9:10 Opening exercises.
9:10 to 9:40 Arithmetic, Class 1. Arith., Class 2.
9:40 to 10:10 Arithmetic, Class 2 Geog., Class 1.
10:10 to 10:30 Drawing.
10:30 to 10:45 Recess.
10:45 to 11:10 Language, Class 1. Geog., Class 2.
11:10 to 11:35 Language, Class 2. Arith., Class 1.
11:35 to 12:00 Geography, Class 1. Arith., Class 2.

P. M.

1:30 to 1:55 Reading, Class 2. Lg. or rd., Cl. 1.
1:55 to 2:20 Reading, Class 1. Lg. or rd., Cl. 2.
2:20 to 2:45 Writing.
2:45 to 3:00 Recess.
3:00 to 3:15 Spelling.
3:15 to 3:40 Geography, Class 2. Arith., Class 1.
3:40 to 4:00 Music.

SIXTH AND SEVENTH GRADES
A. M.

	RECITATIONS.	STUDY.

9:00 to 9:10 Opening exercises.
9:10 to 9:40 Arithmetic, Class 1. Arith., Class 2.

	RECITATIONS.	STUDY.
9:40 to 10:05	Reading, Class 2.	Geog., Class 1.
10:05 to 10:30	Reading, Class 1.	Geog., Class 2.
10:30 to 10:45	Recess.	
10:45 to 11:05	Spelling.	
11:05 to 11:40	Arithmetic, Class 2.	Lang., Class 1.
11:40 to 12:00	Music.	

P. M.

1:30 to 1:55	Geography, Class 1.	Lang., Class 2.
1:55 to 2:20	Geography, Class 2.	Read'g, Class 1.
2:20 to 2:45	Writing.	
2:45 to 3:00	Recess.	
3:00 to 3:30	Language, Class 1.	Read'g, Class 2.
3:30 to 4:00	Language, Class 2.	Arith., Class 1.

EIGHTH GRADE.

A. M.

	RECITATIONS.	STUDY.
9:00 to 9:10	Opening exercises.	
9:10 to 9:25	Spelling.	
9:25 to 9:55	Language, Class 1.	History, Class 2.
9:55 to 10:30	Language, Class 2.	History, Class 1.
10:30 to 10:45	Recess.	
10:45 to 11:20	Arithmetic, Class 1.	Lang., Class 2.
11:20 to 12:00	Arithmetic, Class 2.	Lang., Class 1.

P. M.

1:30 to 2:10	History, Class 1.	Arith., Class 2.
2:10 to 2:45	History, Class 2.	Arith., Class 1.

2:45 to 3:00 Recess.
3:00 to 3:40 Reading.
3:40 to 4:00 Music.

NOTES.

Pupils of the first grade have drawing with the general lesson in the forenoon, and with the writing in the afternoon.

Pupils of the sixth grade take drawing twice a week in place of writing, and once a week at the option of the teacher.

Pupils of the seventh grade have drawing three times a week in place of writing.

Pupils of the eighth grade have drawing twice a week in place of reading.

During the last half of the eighth year, physiology is studied in place of history.

During the last quarter of the seventh year, history is taken in place of geography.

The work in science is included in the general lesson in grades 1, 2 and 3, and in language in grades 4 and 5.

In case there are two grades in one room, the programme assigned to the higher grade should be followed for both.